COLORING

IS A GREAT WAY TO

RELAX, ESCAPE

AND

CREATE

This book was created with YOU in mind.

When you need to get away...*COLOR!*

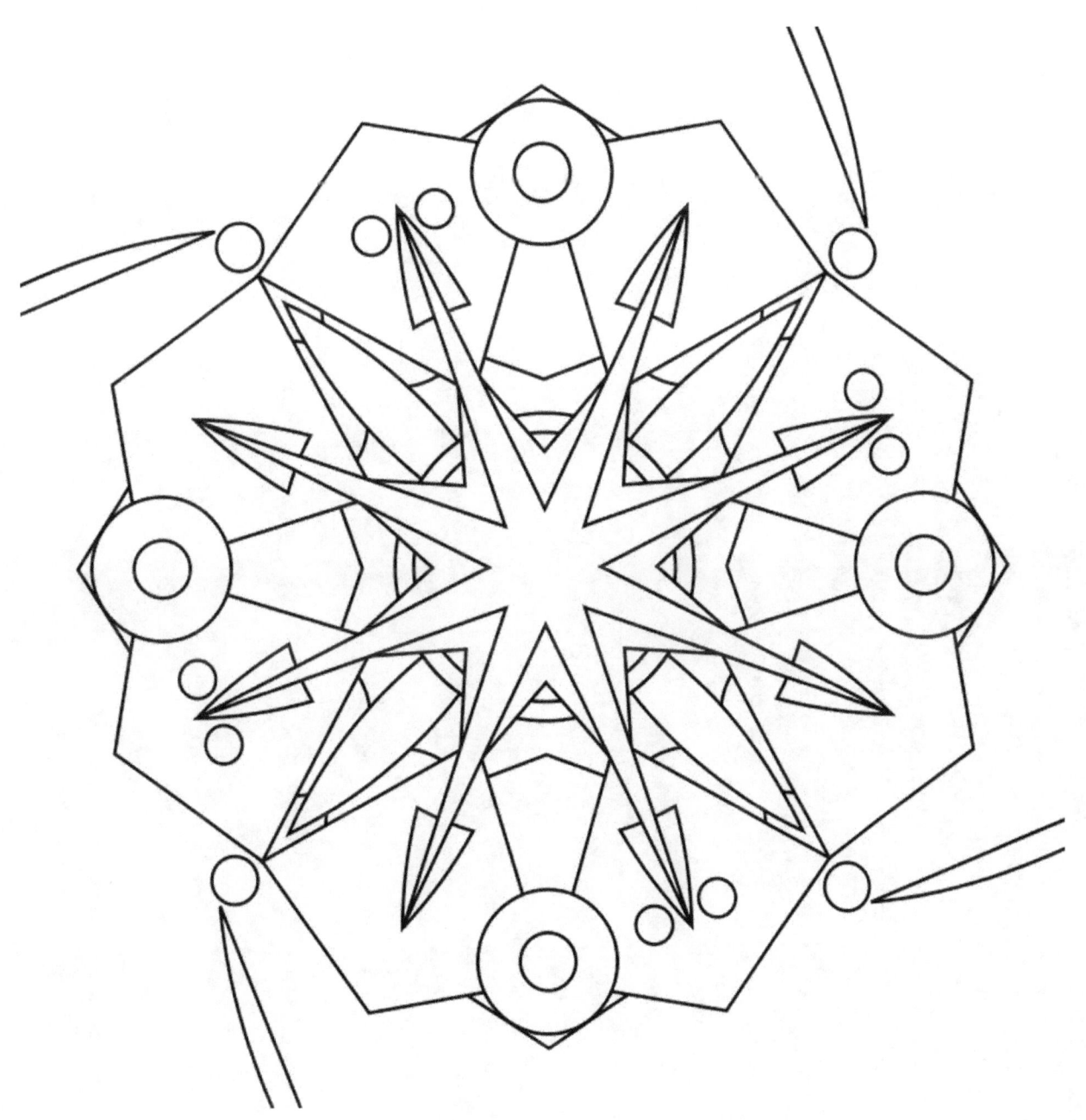

This book is dedicated to

Miriam Vinton

who has, and always will inspire me.

Coming soon is the Little Red Shirt coloring book which is a companion to the Kindle book of the same title.

Also, soon to arrive are Volumes 1 of the Zirkel Series and the Stoner Series.

Email: favoritesofruthies@gmail.com

Join me on my Facebook Group:

Coloring Designs

Welcome to Book Three of the Mandala Series!

This book has more intricate designs. As with my other books you might want to put a blank piece of paper or thin cardboard behind the design before you begin to color. This will catch any bleed through colors and provide a place for you to make notes if you wish. I find sometimes that I need to write down the color I use so if I want to use it again I don't have to search through all pencils or markers that are laying all over my work space.

There are many mediums you can use to color. I suggest using markers, colored pencils, gel pens, or watercolor pencils.

If you like, you can share your colored pages on my FaceBook page called Coloring Designs.

Every master piece you create will look different. Enjoy!

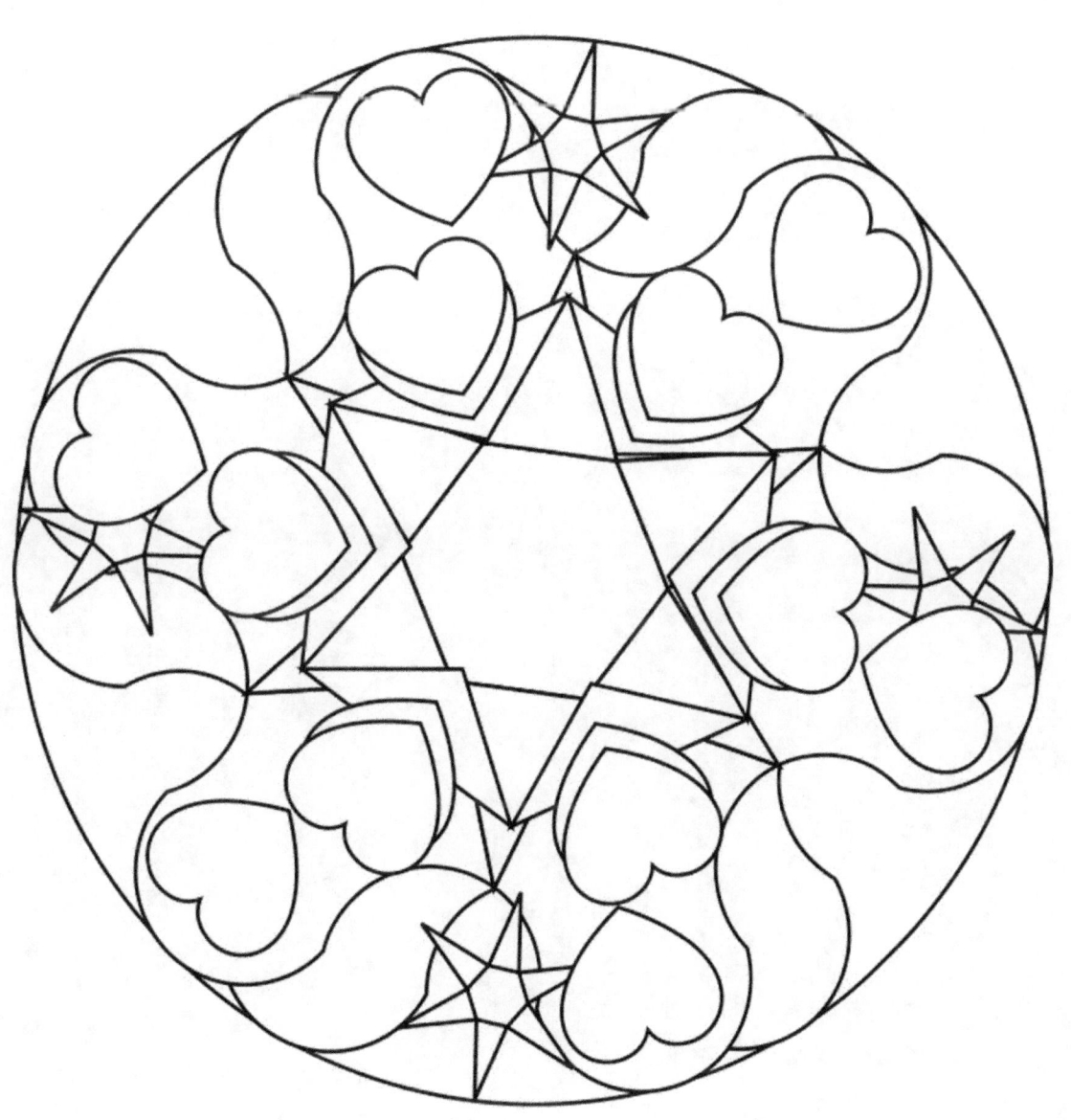

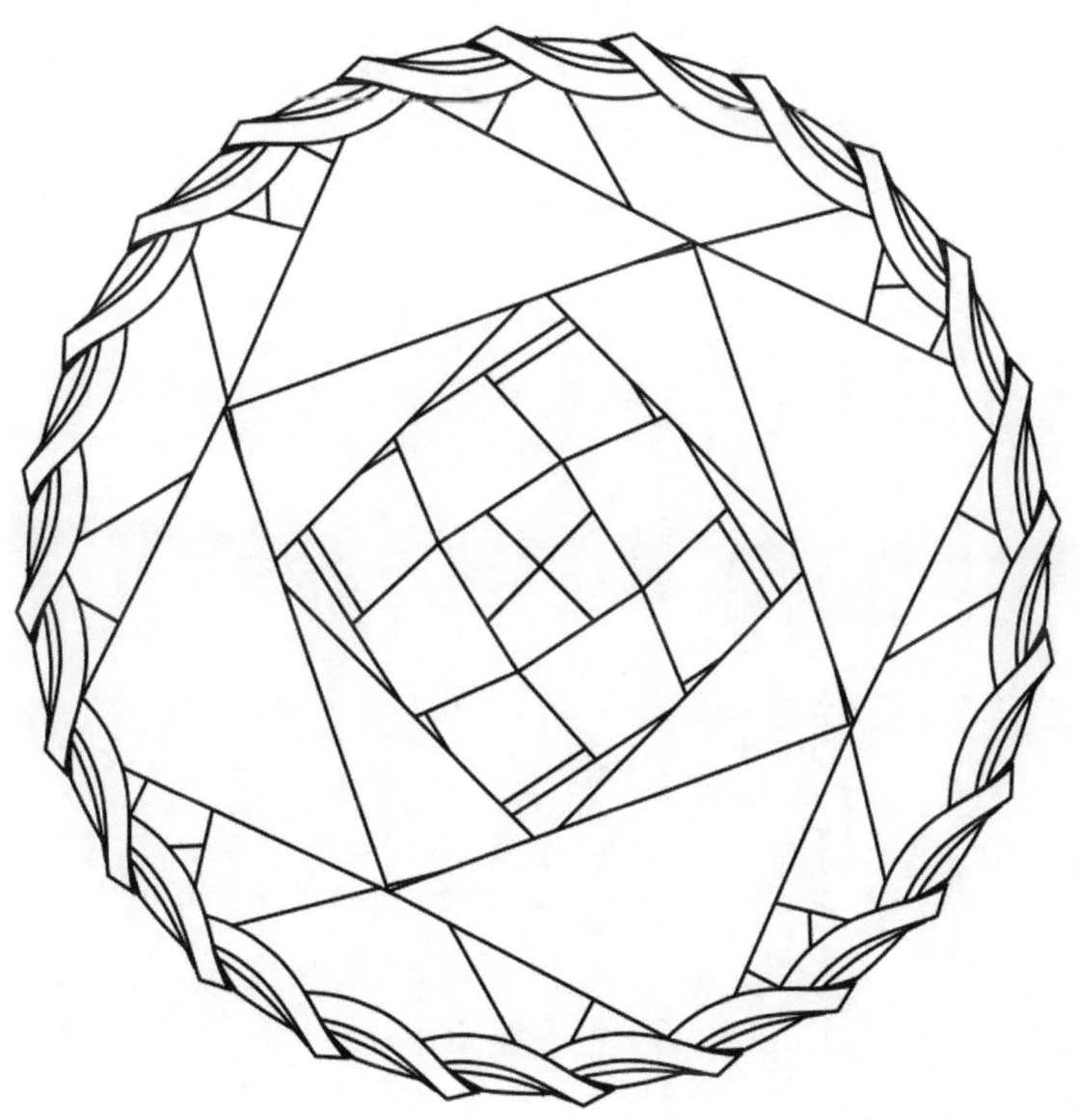

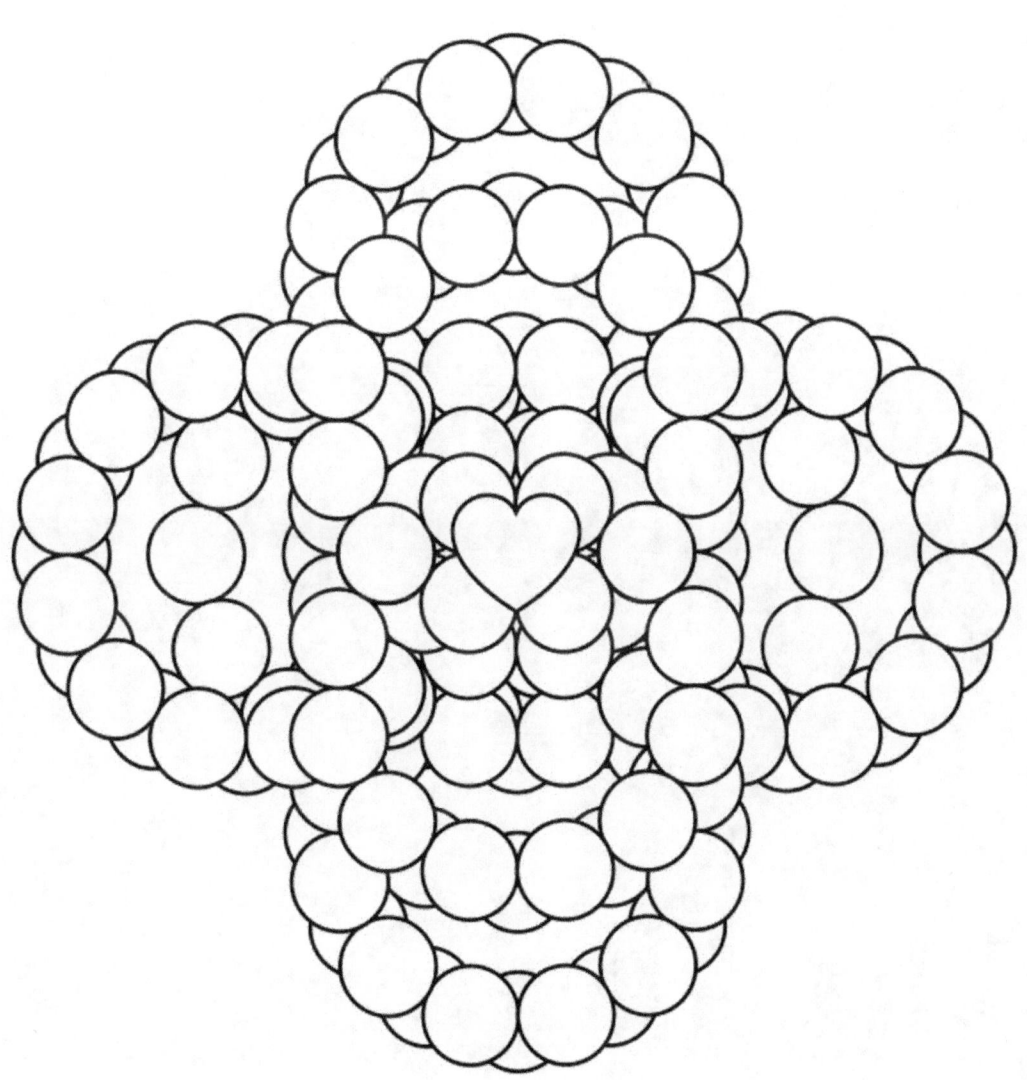

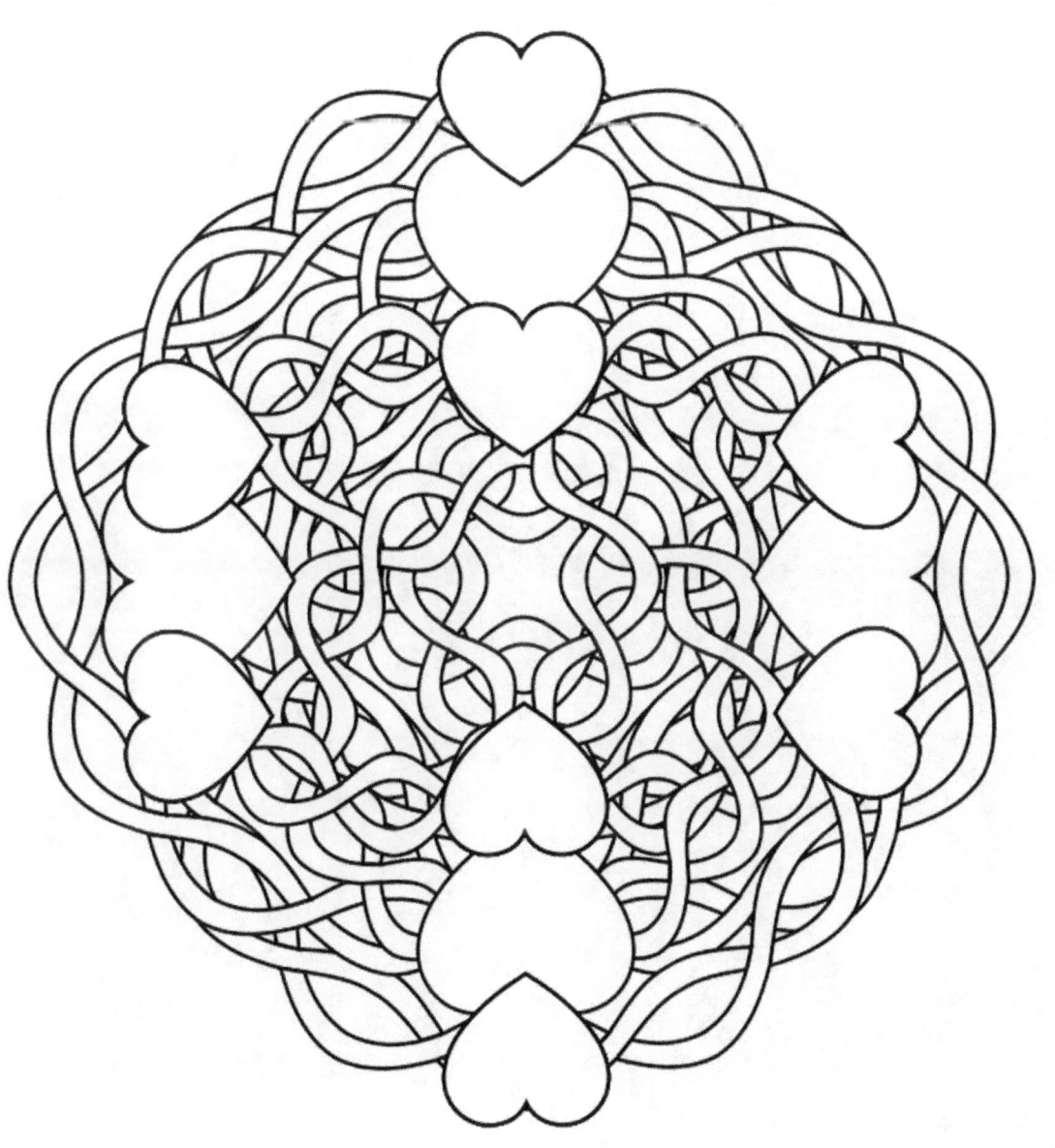

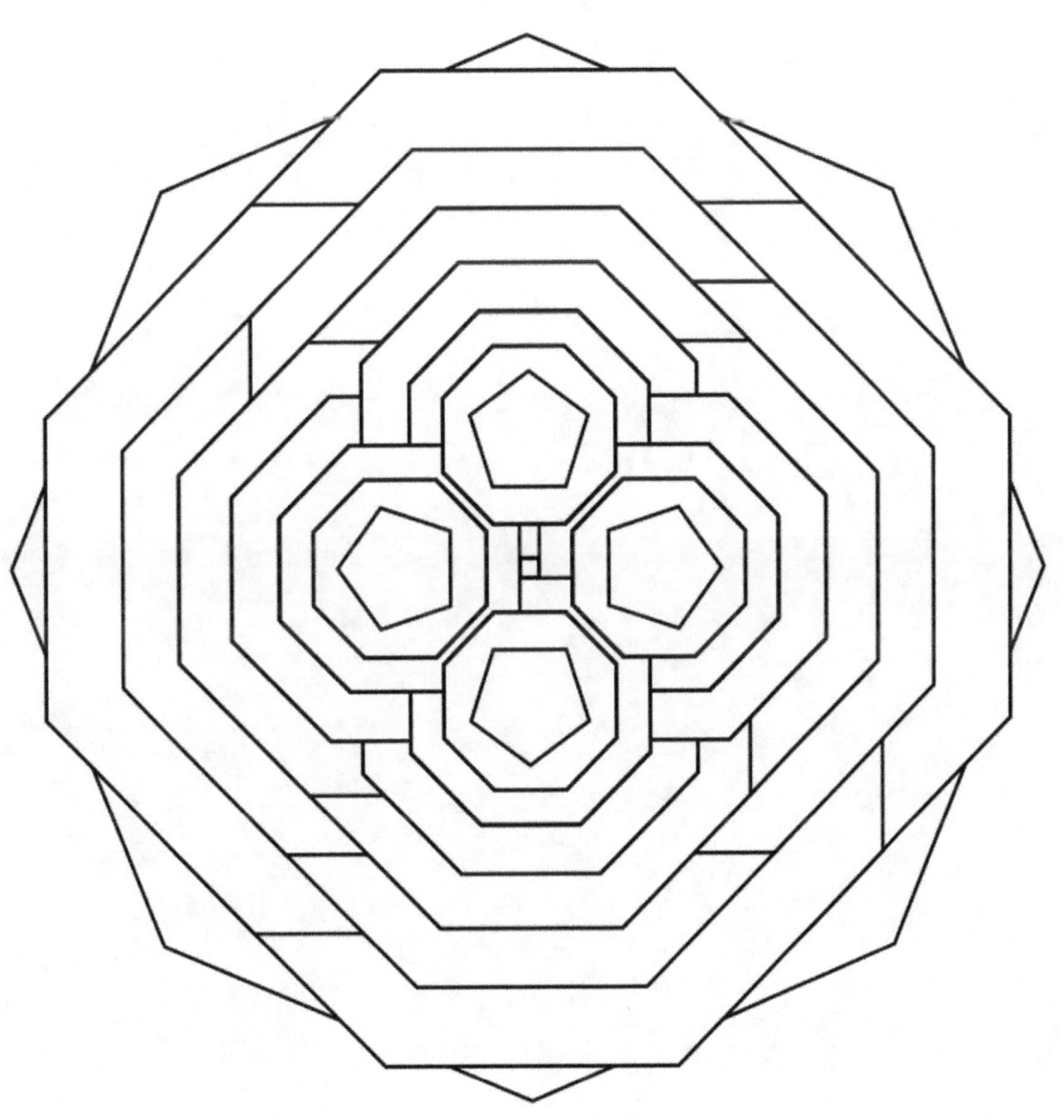

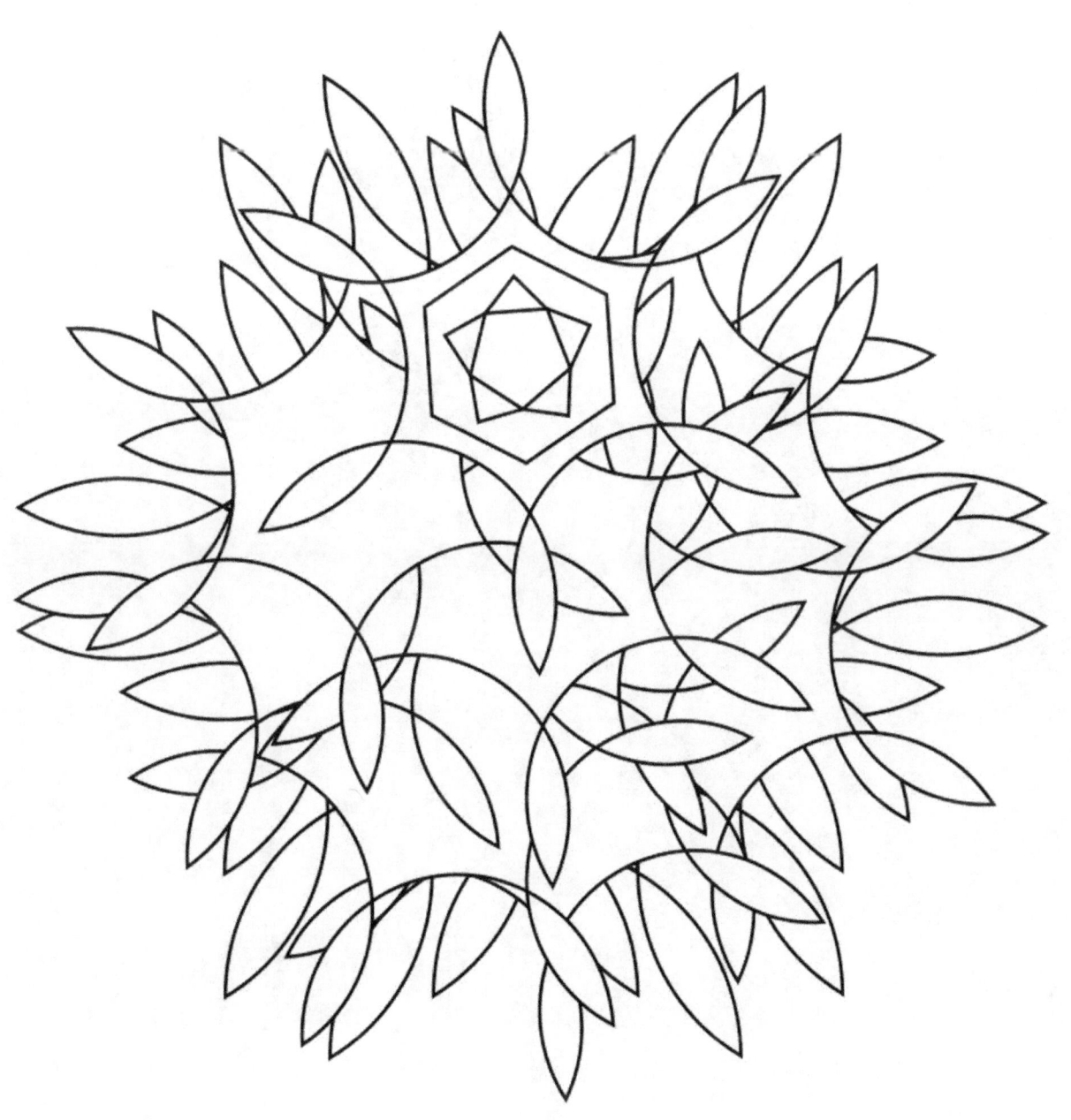

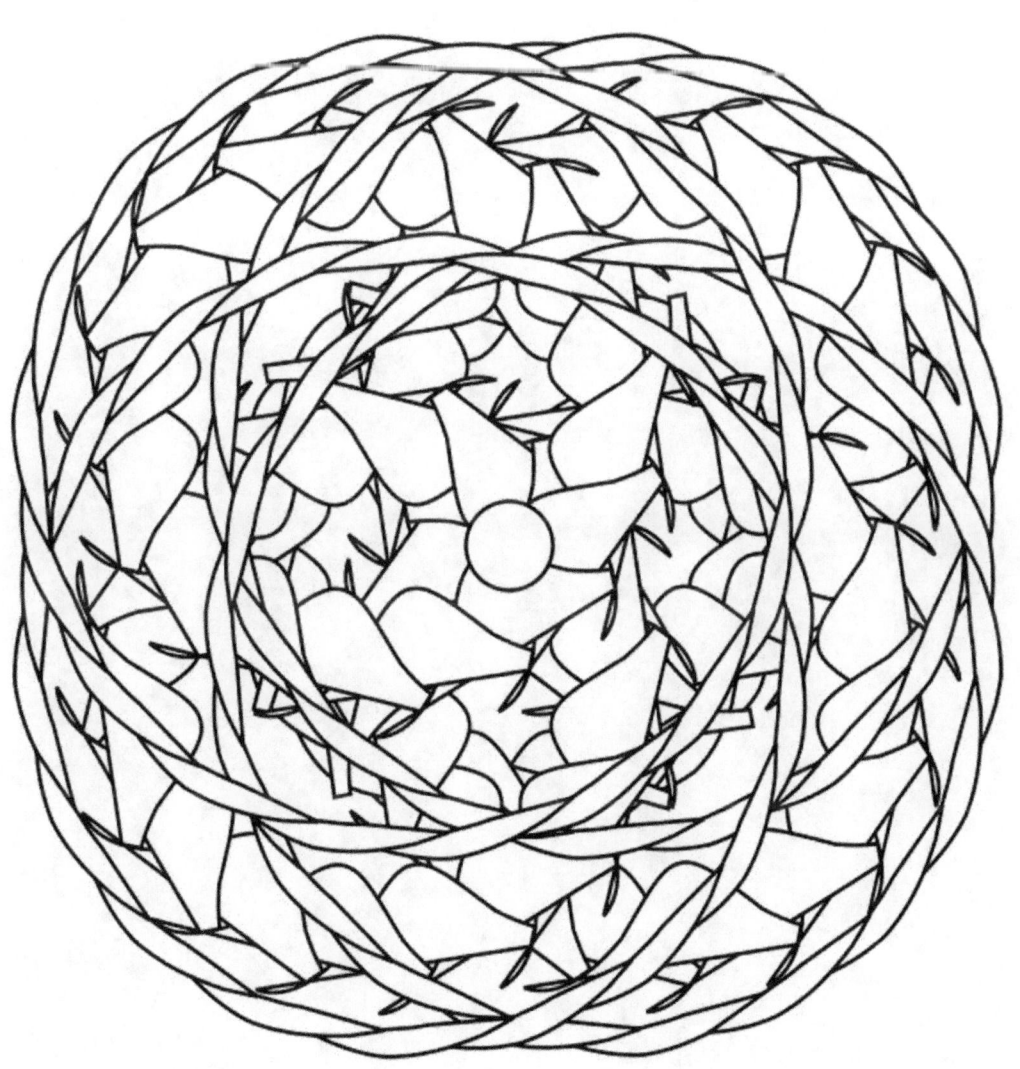

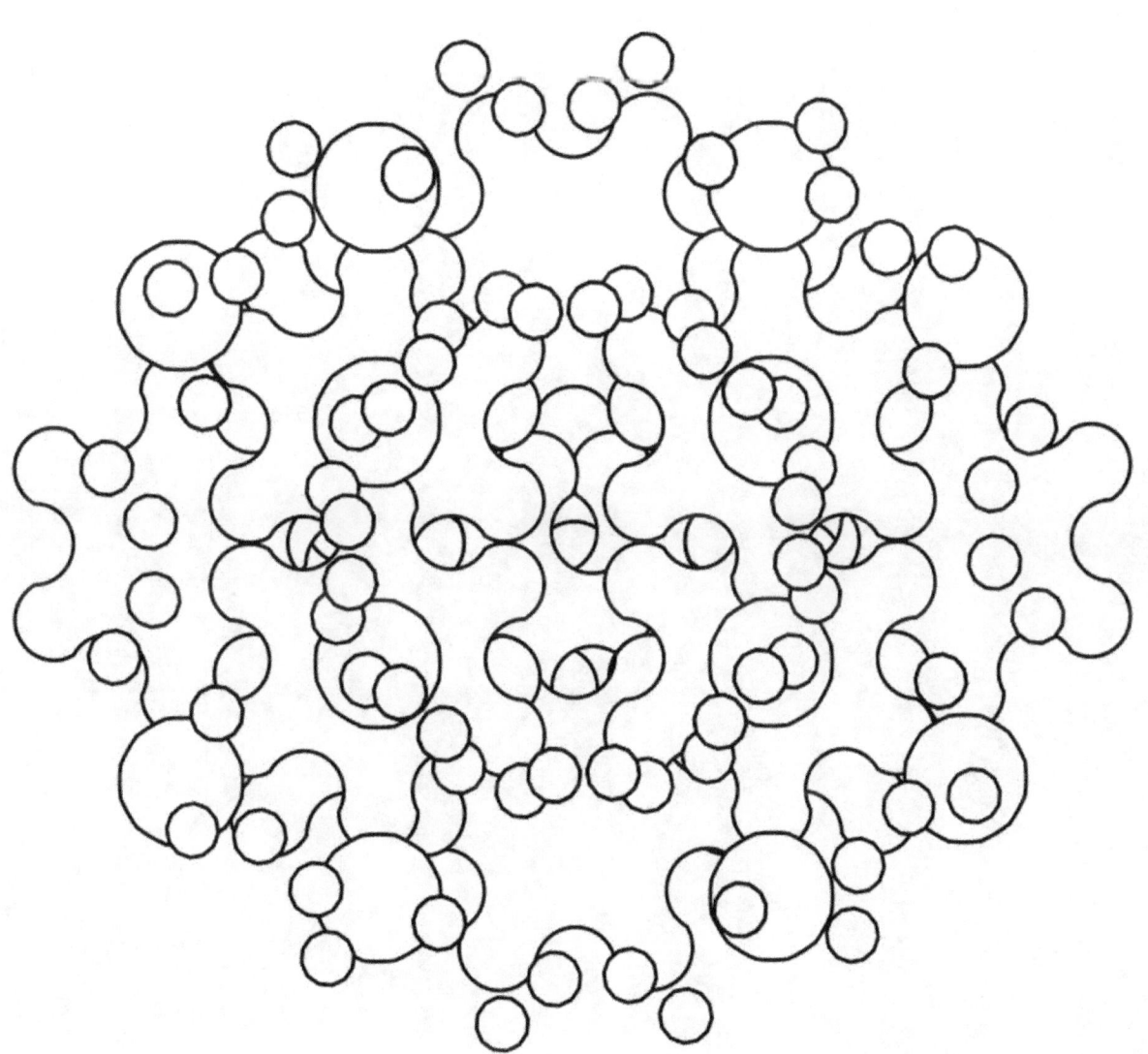

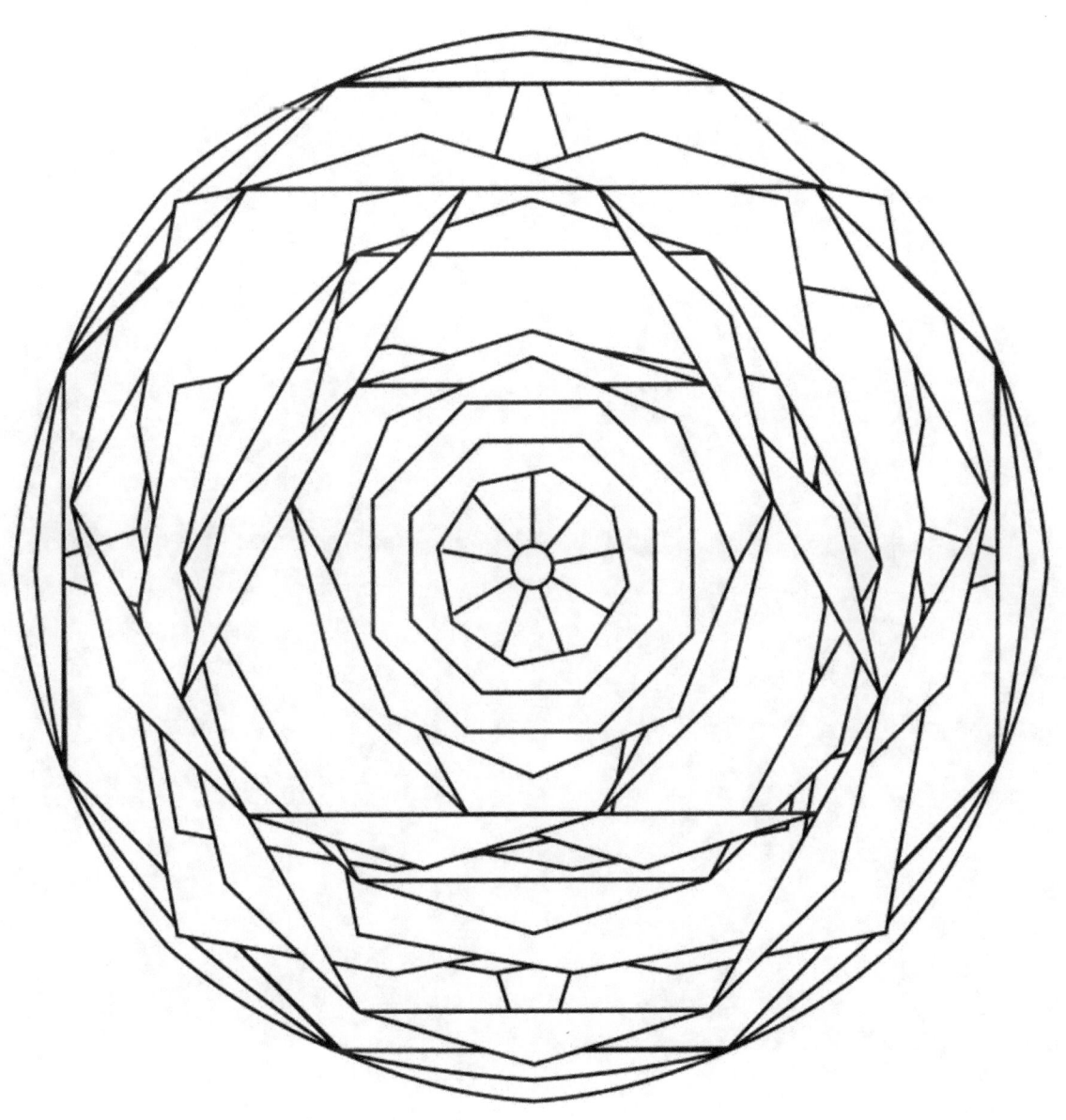

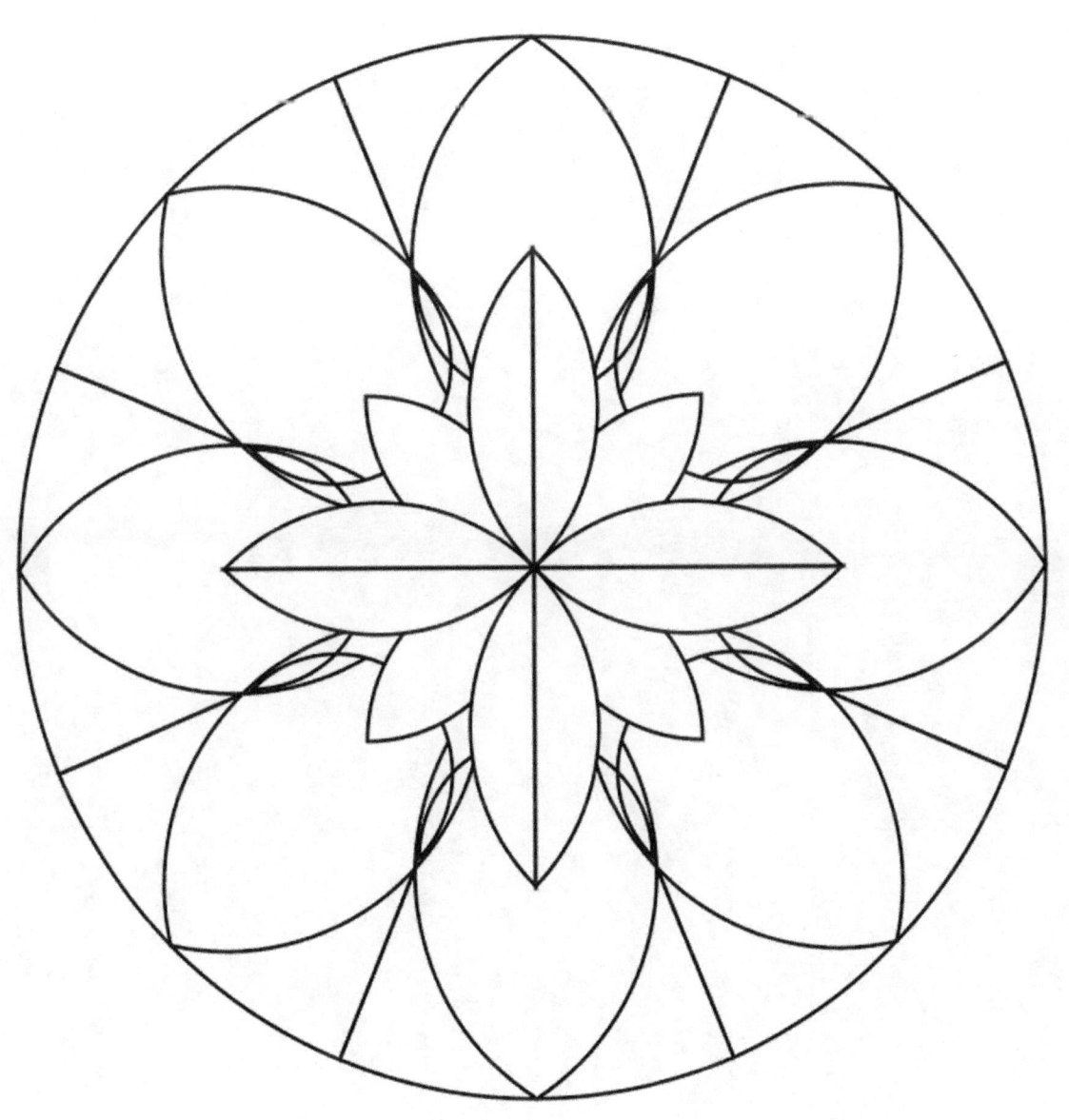

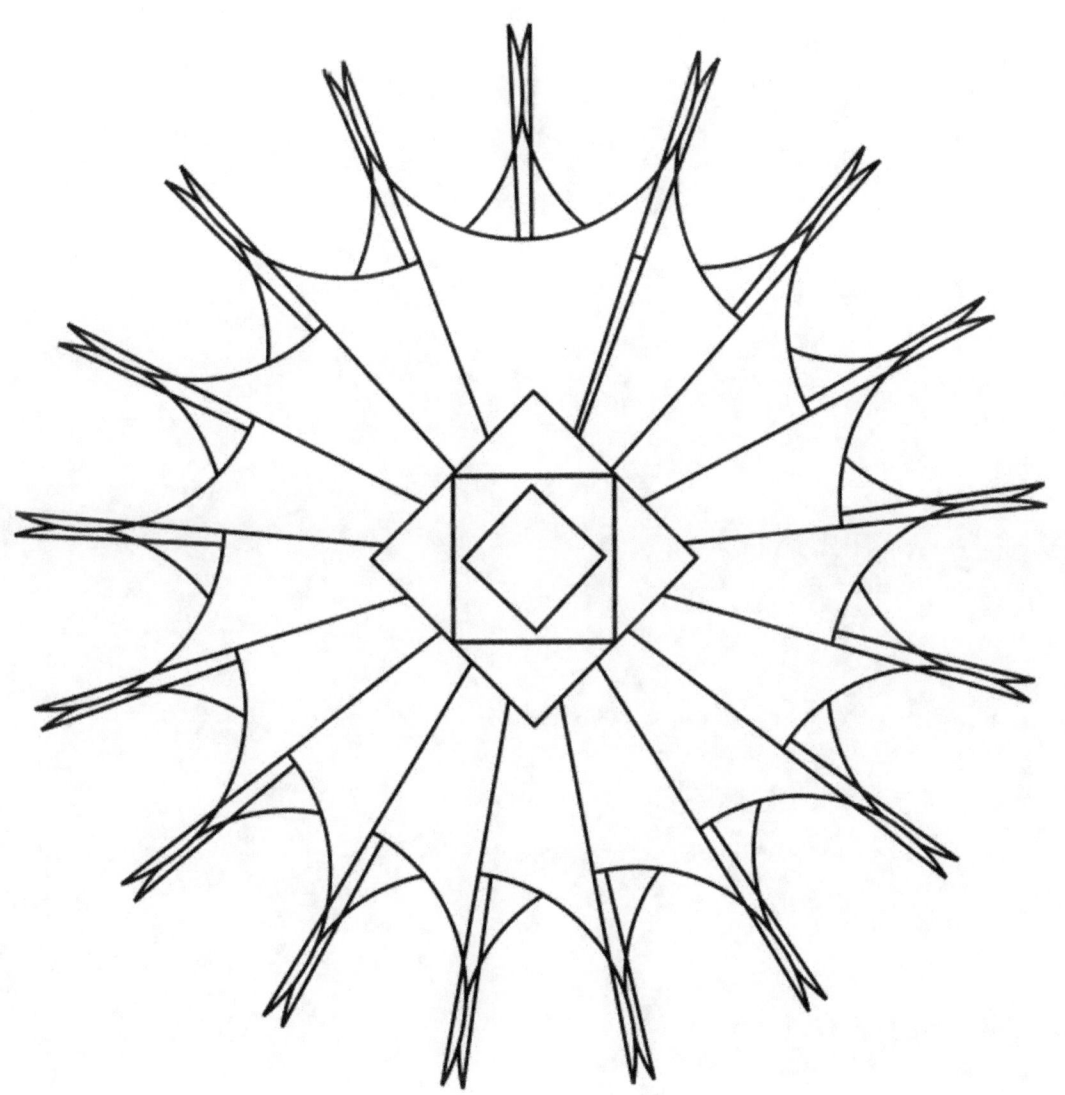

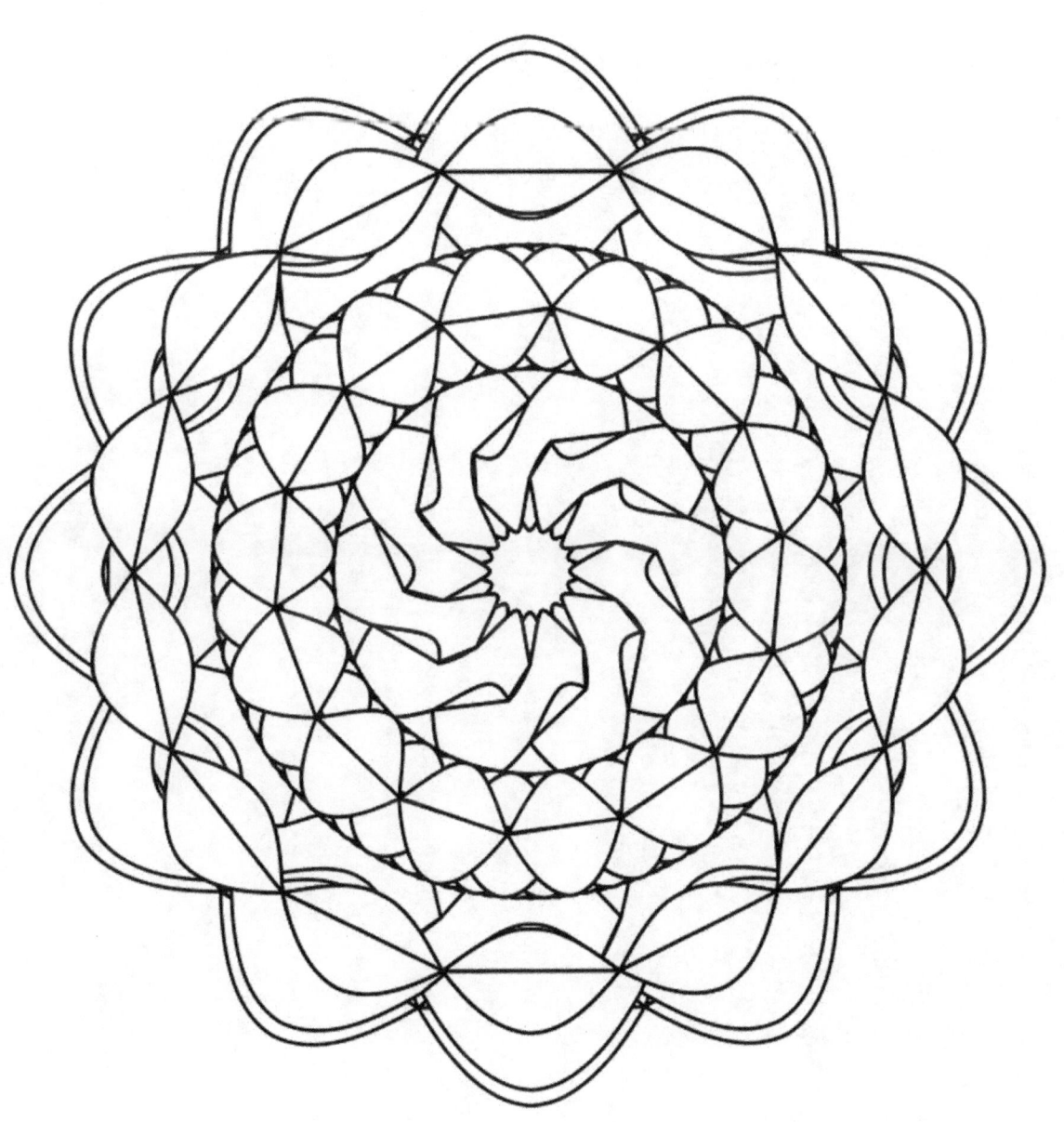

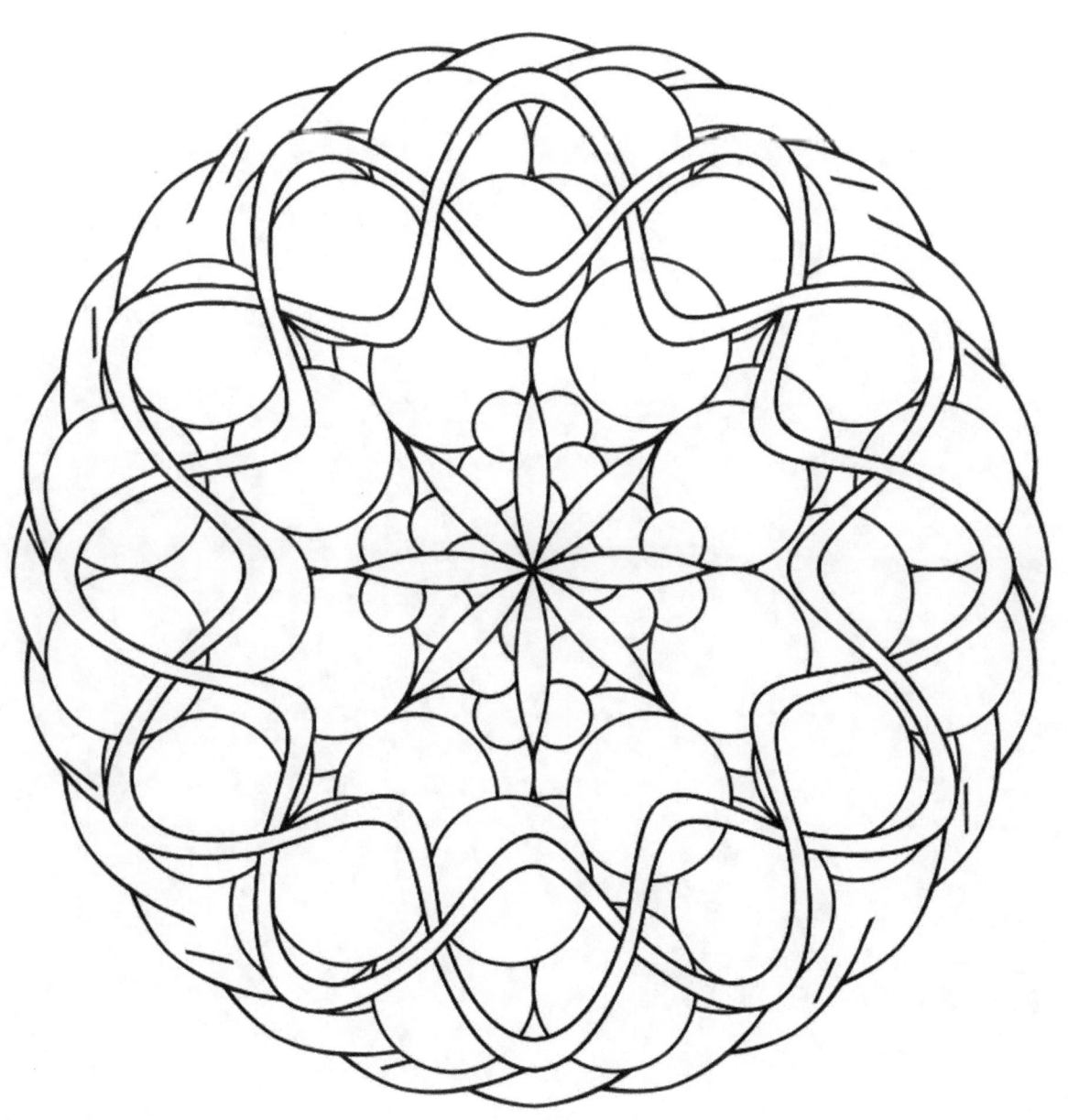

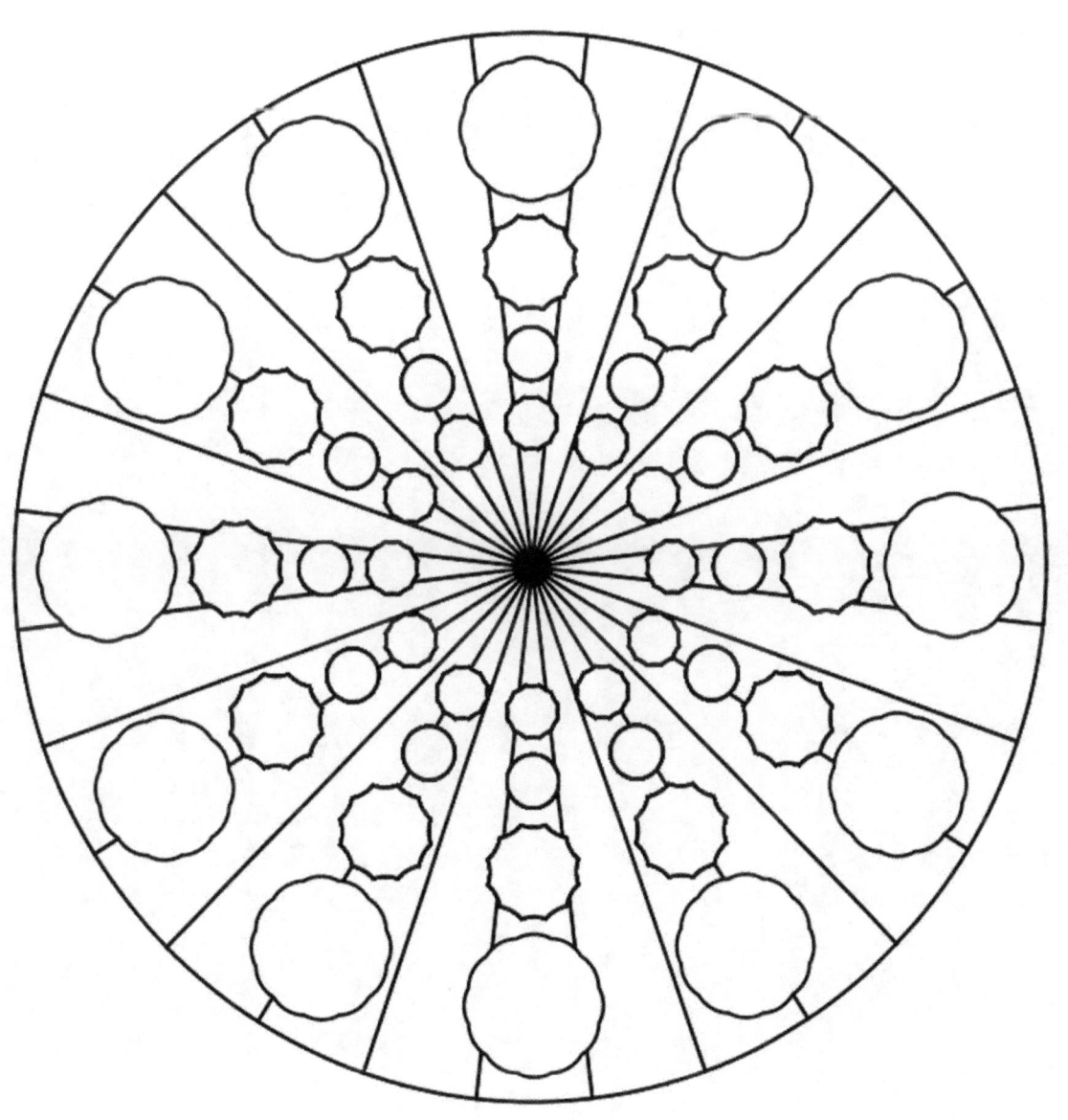

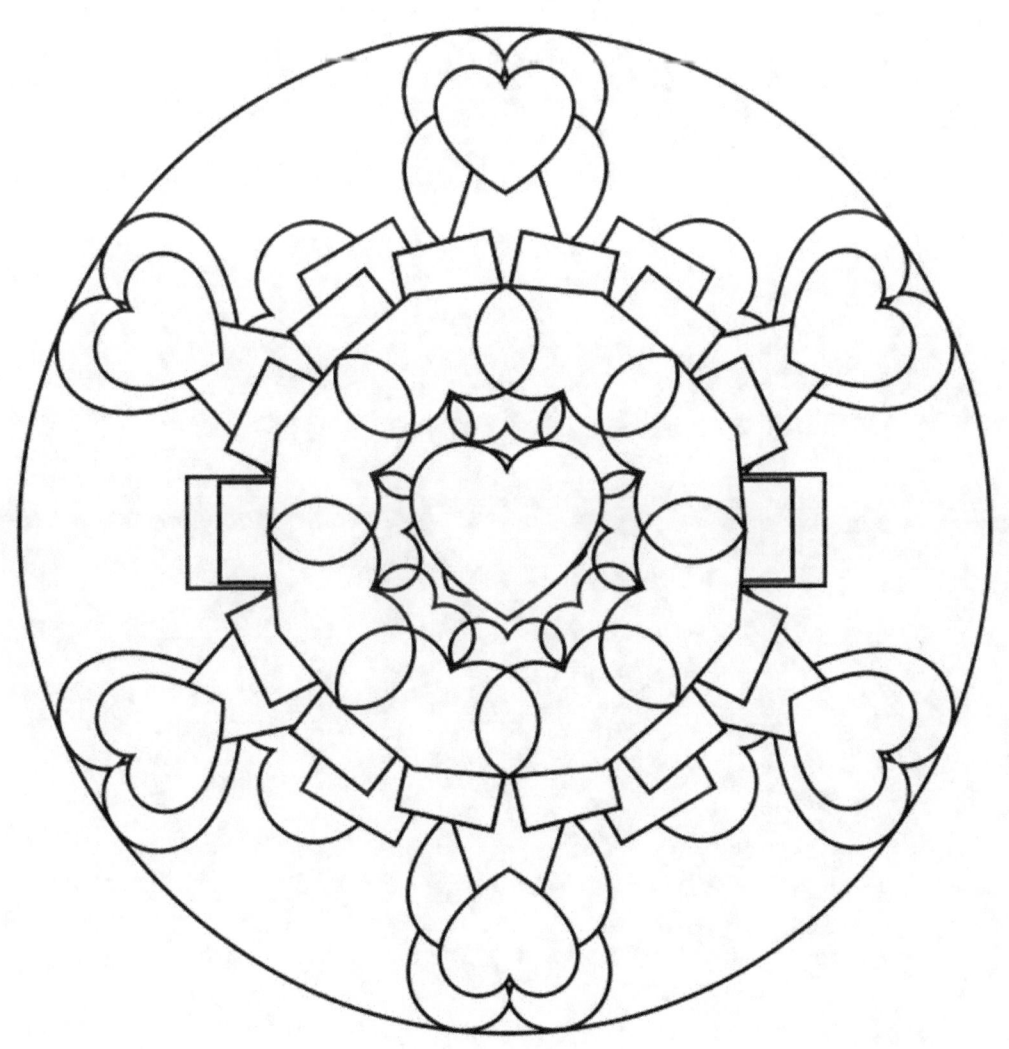

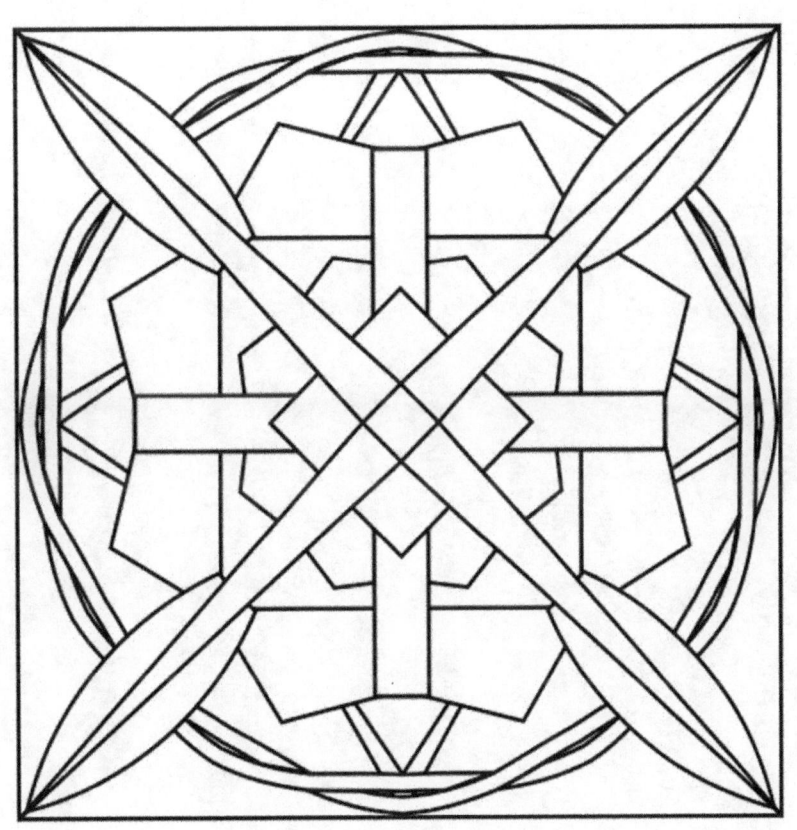

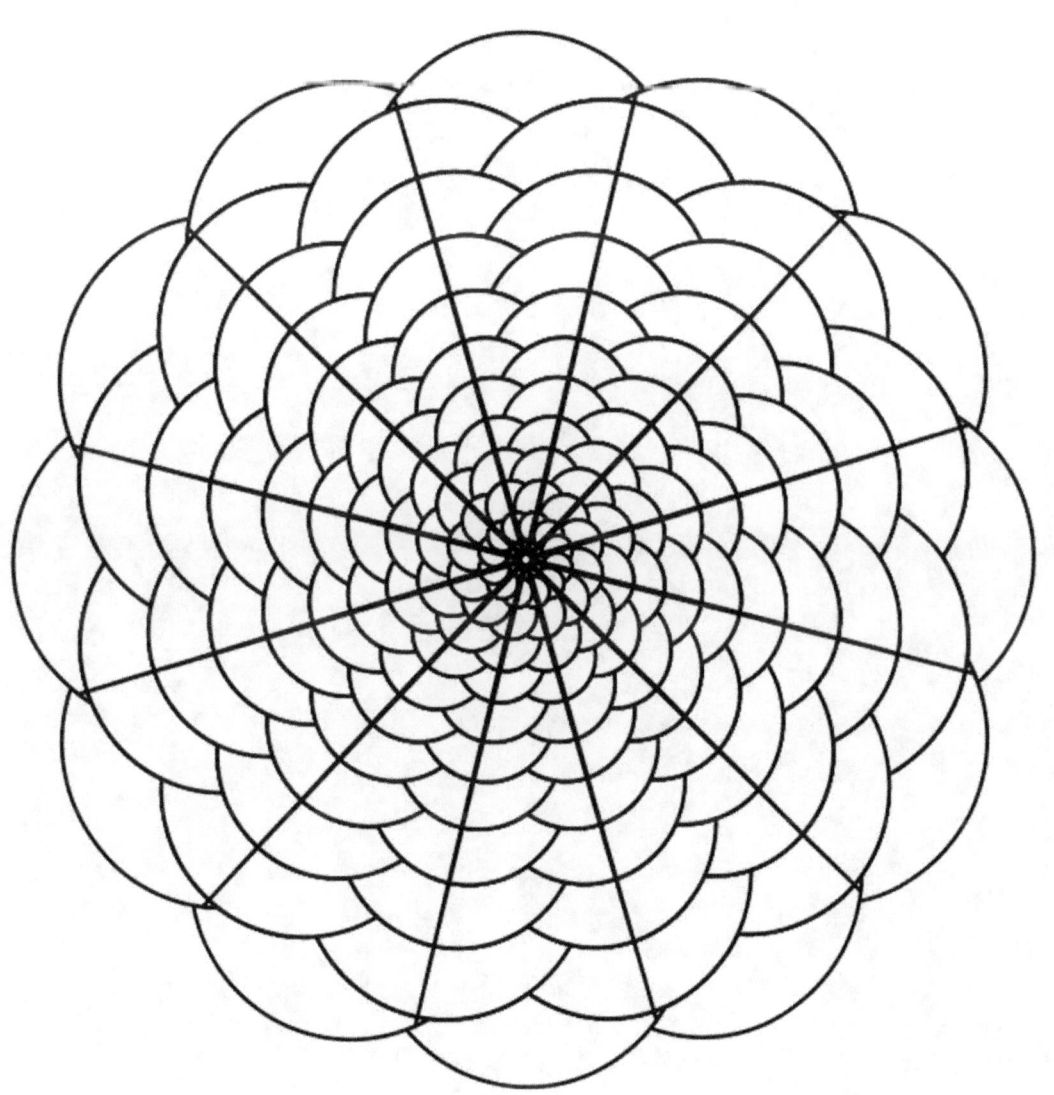

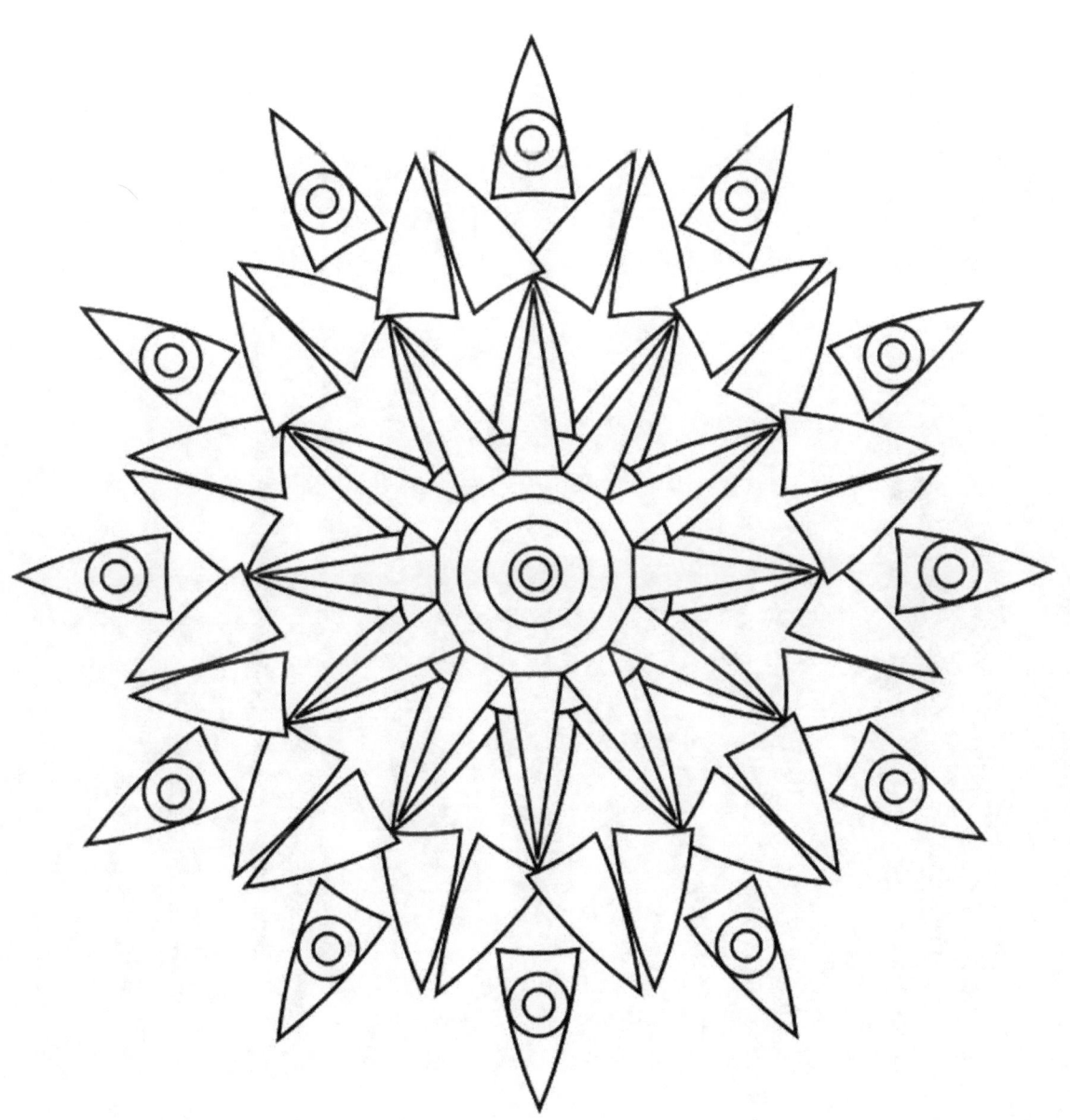

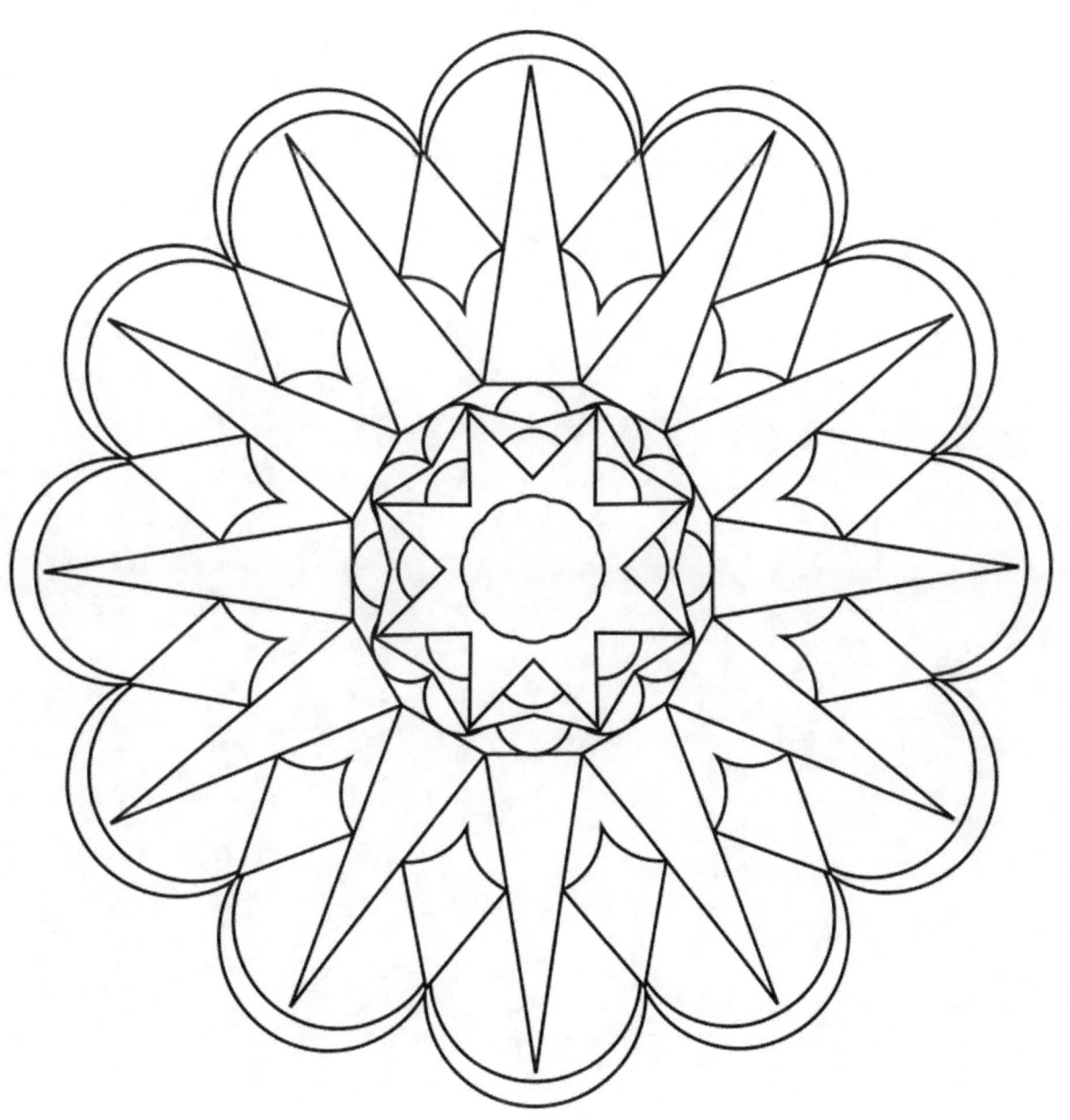

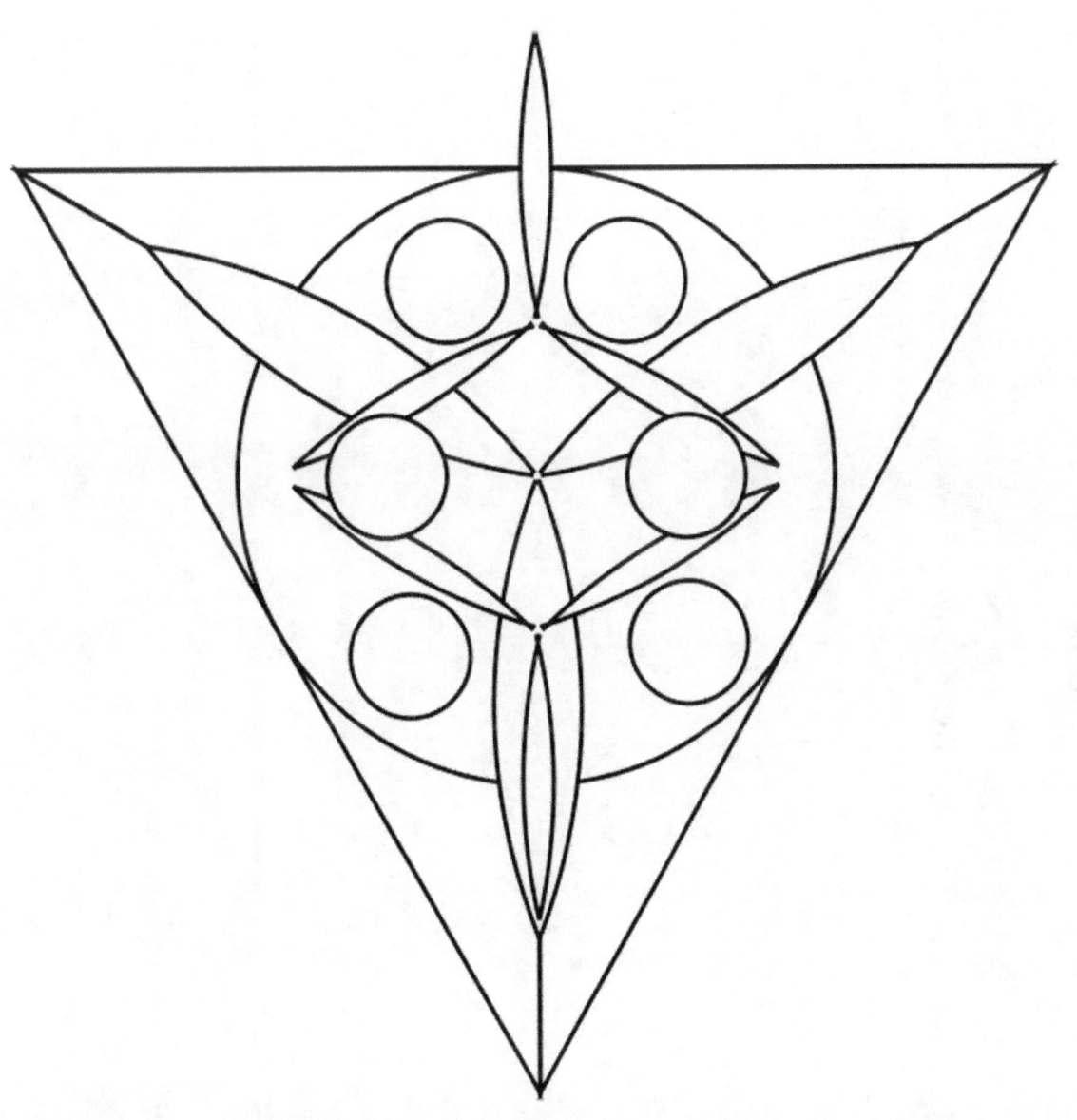

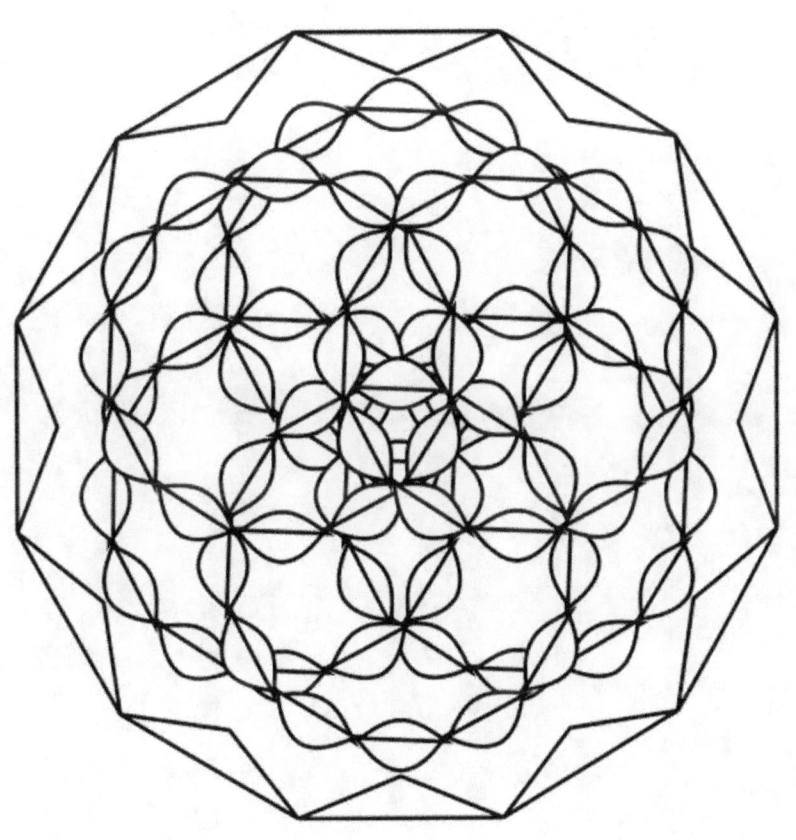

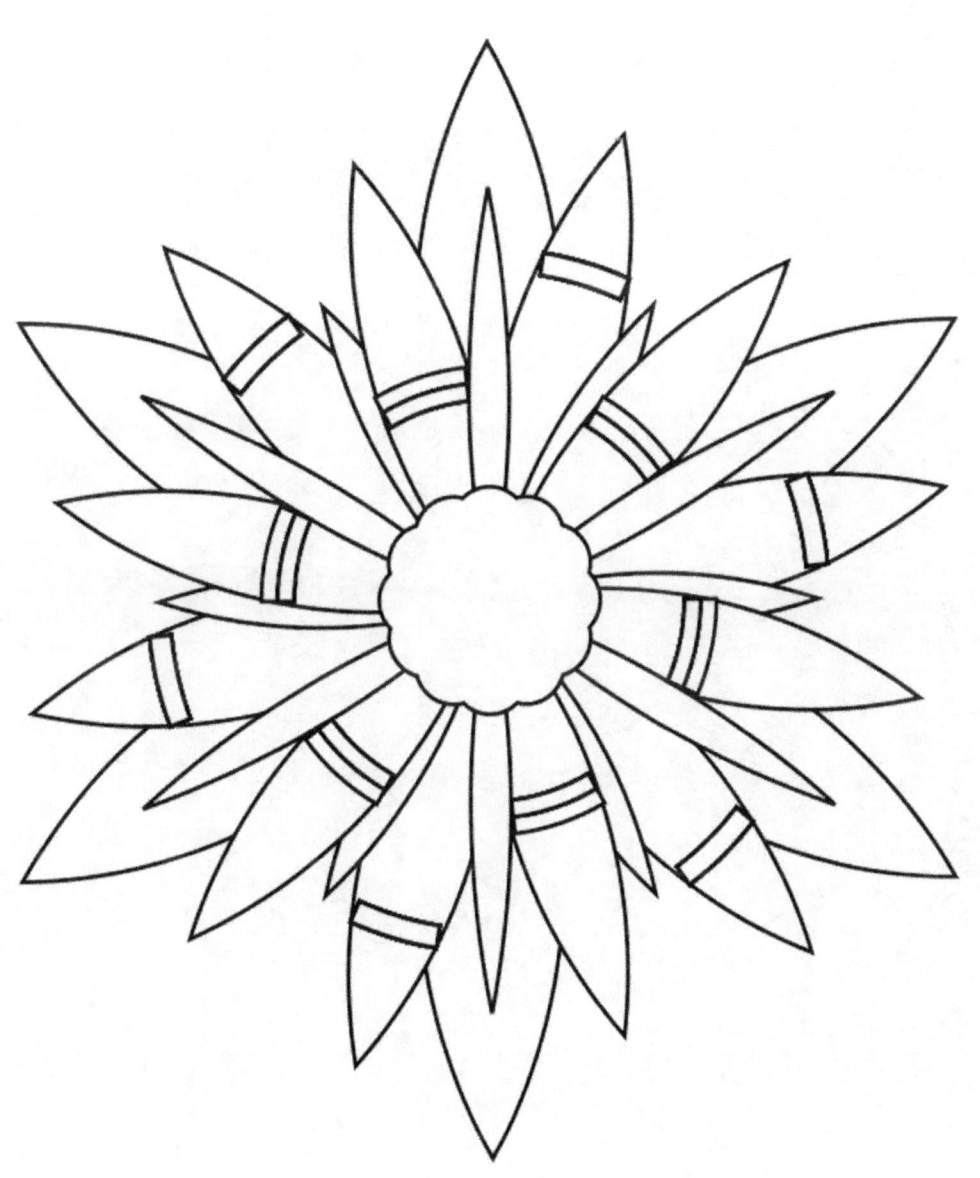